German For The American Soldier

You are holding a reproduction of an original work that is in the public domain in the United States of America, and possibly other countries. You may freely copy and distribute this work as no entity (individual or corporate) has a copyright on the body of the work. This book may contain prior copyright references, and library stamps (as most of these works were scanned from library copies). These have been scanned and retained as part of the historical artifact.

This book may have occasional imperfections such as missing or blurred pages, poor pictures, errant marks, etc. that were either part of the original artifact, or were introduced by the scanning process. We believe this work is culturally important, and despite the imperfections, have elected to bring it back into print as part of our continuing commitment to the preservation of printed works worldwide. We appreciate your understanding of the imperfections in the preservation process, and hope you enjoy this valuable book.

GERMAN FOR THE AMERICAN SOLDIER

WITH VOCABULARY

BY

THEODORE B. HEWITT
Assistant Professor, Williams College

AND

HOLLON A. FARR
Assistant Professor, Yale College

HARVARD COLLEGE LIBRARY
GIFT OF
PROF. WILLIAM G. HOWARD
July 5, 1935

COPYRIGHT, 1918,
BY
T. B. HEWITT
AND
H. A. FARR

PREFACE

ALTHOUGH this book presupposes on the part of the user some knowledge of the elements of German grammar, it is quite possible that it might be studied with profit by those who have had no previous instruction in German.

The purpose of the text is to furnish in convenient form phrases and sentences that will be helpful to the American soldier in his dealings with German prisoners and with German-speaking civilians on German territory. It also affords a knowledge of the ordinary military vocabulary that will assist in the interpretation of intercepted documents and despatches.

Exercises I to X are based on the more general vocabulary, while Exercises XI to XX deal more specifically with technical military phraseology.

For purposes of drill most of the exercises are supplemented by sentences to be translated from English into German.

The vocabulary contains about 450 of the more unusual words and phrases.

T. B. HEWITT
H. A. FARR

NEW HAVEN, CONN.
MAY, 1918

CONTENTS

		PAGE
I.	General Introductory Matter	2
II.	Practical Study of German; Interpretation of a Letter	6
III.	Inquiring the Way; Journey; Purchases; Meals; Billeting.	8
IV.	Health; Hospital; Diseases.	14
V.	Ambulance; Medicine.	18
VI.	Orders and Commands; Instructions to Prisoners	20
VII.	Questioning Prisoners	24
VIII.	Questioning Prisoners (*continued*); Confiscated Diary.	28
IX.	Campaign; A New Offensive; Bombardment; Air Attack.	30
X.	Intercepted Despatches; Reports of an Action.	34
XI.	Attack on a Fortified City.	38
XII.	Uniforms; Weapons; Billets.	42
XIII.	Airplanes and Airships.	46
XIV.	Navy.	50
XV.	Firing Data.	54
XVI.	Merchant Marine; Blockade; Submarines	58
XVII.	Heavy and Light Artillery.	62
XVIII.	Infantry.	66
XIX.	Military Rank.	70
XX.	Maps; Military Information.	74
	Vocabulary	78

I

1. Good morning. Is Mr. N. in?
2. Yes indeed. Please be seated. You come just in time.
3. Introduce me to this gentleman. His name is Mr. B.
4. Can he speak German? Yes, he speaks very fluently.
5. What is that in German?
6. I beg pardon. I did not understand. Will you not speak more slowly, please.
7. What's the matter? What are you reading in your newspaper?
8. According to a despatch from R. the whole region of N. has been placed under martial law.
9. I can readily believe that. Probably however the despatch was delayed. We ought to have known that three days ago.
10. I believe the situation is growing more threatening day by day.
11. You are right.
12. I read day before yesterday in the paper that the Insurgents have been bombarding the capital. Do you believe that?
13. I attach no importance to it.
14. On the contrary there probably exists unheard of disorder in the whole country.
15. It will be a long time before that happens.

I

1. Guten Morgen! Ist Herr N. zu sprechen?
2. Jawohl! Bitte nehmen Sie Platz! Sie kommen eben recht.
3. Machen Sie mich mit diesem Herrn bekannt. Er heiszt Herr B.
4. Kann er Deutsch sprechen? Ja, er spricht sehr geläufig.
5. Wie heiszt das auf Deutsch?
6. Ich bitte um Verzeihung. Ich habe nicht verstanden. Wollen Sie nicht langsamer sprechen, wenn ich bitten darf.
7. Was ist los? Was lesen Sie in Ihrer Zeitung?
8. Laut einer Depesche aus R. ist der ganze Bezirk von N. unter Kriegsrecht gestellt worden.
9. Das glaube ich gern. Die Depesche wurde aber wohl verzögert. Das hätten wir schon vor drei Tagen wissen sollen.
10. Ich glaube, die Lage gestaltet sich von Tag zu Tag drohender.
11. Sie haben recht.
12. Ich habe vorgestern in der Zeitung gelesen, dasz die Insurgenten die Hauptstadt beschossen haben. Glauben Sie das?
13. Ich lege kein Gewicht darauf.
14. Im Gegenteil herrscht wohl im ganzen Lande unerhörte Unordnung.
15. Das liegt noch in weiter Ferne.

16. I am not of your opinion. Let's drop the subject however, if you are agreeable.//
17. What time is it?//
18. It is only half past three.//
19. Already half past three? It is later than I thought. My watch is slow.//
20. It is still early. You have plenty of time.

DRILL

1. He introduced me to the gentleman and we sat down. 2. What is the gentleman's name? 3. You speak very fluently. Do you know what this word is in German? 4. I do not understand what you say. 5. Have you read the newspaper? 6. I read yesterday that the capital was placed under martial law. Do you believe that? 7. Day before yesterday the situation was threatening. 8. If it is agreeable to you, I will read (vor-lesen) you this letter. 9. I have no time as it is very late. 10. Your watch is fast (vor-gehen). It is only half past eight. 11. According to my watch it is already a quarter to nine (drei Viertel neun). 12. I think you are right.

16. Ich bin nicht Ihrer Ansicht. Reden wir aber nicht mehr davon, wenn es Ihnen so recht ist.

17. Wie viel Uhr ist es?

18. Es ist erst halb vier.

19. Schon halb vier? Es ist später als ich dachte. Meine Uhr geht nach.

20. Es ist noch früh. Sie haben noch viel Zeit.

Additional Notes

II

1. Why are you studying German?
2. I shall probably have to talk with German prisoners "over there".
3. Your knowledge will enable you therefore to make yourself understood and to translate intercepted letters. I must praise your diligence.
4. Do you know, a friend of mine recently recommended to his students some German pamphlets on X-rays. Since the students didn't know any German they could not translate these pamphlets and could therefore make no use of them.
5. That was stupid. Why should we bite off our noses to spite our faces?
6. Let's rather continue to study German.
7. Yes. I am convinced that greater linguistic knowledge is going to enable us to grow up to more useful citizens and also to more efficient soldiers.
8. For example, could you translate this letter?
9. I will at least make the attempt. Where did you pick it up?
10. That is immaterial. How does the letter read?
11. Here's something interesting:—
"Last month 500 ships sailed from the port of B. The whole region of N. has been placed under martial law. We shall extort money in R. and thus be able to defray the war expenses. 500,000 men are now fully equipped. Mobilization is to follow on the first of June. The first attack we shall make near S."

II

1. Warum treiben (*or* lernen) Sie Deutsch?
2. Ich werde wohl "da drüben" mit deutschen Gefangenen reden müssen.
3. Ihre Kenntnisse werden Sie also befähigen sich verständlich zu machen und aufgefangene Briefe zu übersetzen. Ich musz Ihren Fleisz loben.
4. Wissen Sie, ein Freund von mir hat neulich seinen Studenten einige deutsche Schriften über die X-Strahlen empfohlen. Da die Studenten kein Deutsch konnten, konnten sie diese Schriften nicht übersetzen, und also keinen Gebrauch davon machen.
5. Das war dumm. Warum sollten wir uns ins Gesicht schlagen?
6. Fahren wir lieber fort, Deutsch zu treiben.
7. Ja. Ich bin überzeugt, dasz grössere Sprachkenntnisse uns befähigen werden, zu nützlicheren Bürgern so wie auch zu tüchtigern Soldaten heranzuwachsen.
8. Könnten Sie zum Beispiel diesen Brief übersetzen?
9. Ich will wenigstens den Versuch machen. Wo haben Sie ihn aufgefangen?
10. Das tut nichts zur Sache. Wie lautet der Brief?
11. Hier steht etwas Interessantes:—
"Im letzten Monat sind fünf hundert Schiffe aus dem Hafen B. ausgelaufen. Der ganze Bezirk von N. ist unter Kriegsrecht gestellt worden. Wir

DRILL

1. Mr. N. is studying German, because he will probably have to talk with German prisoners "over there." 2. If he can make himself understood he will be an efficient soldier. 3. He will also be able to translate intercepted letters. 4. Can you recommend to me a pamphlet on X-rays? 5. I can make no use of that as I know only a little German. Please translate it for me. 6. I'll translate something from this newspaper. 7. Did you know that in the last month 200 ships sailed from this port? 8. The enemy will

---

III

1. What's the name of this place? I'm an entire stranger here and should like to have a plan and description of the town.

2. Are you familiar with the town and its surroundings?

3. I have lost my way. Where does this street lead to? I want to get to N.

4. Take the second street to the left.

5. Can you take us to N.? Do you know the roads well?

werden in R. Erpressungen ausüben und auf die Weise die Kriegsunkosten bestreiten können. Fünf hundert tausend Mann sind jetzt völlig ausgerüstet. Die Mobilisierung soll am ersten Juni erfolgen. Den ersten Angriff machen wir bei S."

Drill—(continued)

probably extort money in R. 9. In this way they will defray the war expenses. 10. They will put the capital under martial law. 11. Do you know how many thousand men are equipped? 12. When is the mobilization to follow? 13. They will make the first attack near S.

III

1. Wie heiszt dieser Ort? Ich bin hier ganz fremd und möchte einen Plan und eine Beschreibung der Stadt haben.

2. Sind Sie mit der Stadt und deren Umgebung genau bekannt?

3. Ich habe mich verirrt. Wohin führt diese Strasze? Ich will nach N. gehen.

4. Gehen Sie die zweite Strasze links.

5. Können Sie uns nach N. führen? Kennen Sie die Wege genau?

6. I don't know my way around here. I'm looking for the house of the mayor. Is this the right place?

7. No. Don't you see the sign "No Admittance"?

8. Turn to the left, please.

9. I should like to buy some mild cigars, some good tobacco and three boxes of cigarettes.

10. These are very expensive. Have you any cheaper?

11. How much did you say that was?

12. Can you give me change for 10 Marks? No, I have no money with me.

13. Where can one buy maps of the country?

14. At the bookseller's around the corner.

15. I want to speak with the landlord.

16. You must pay in advance. I must insist upon it.

17. What do I owe you?

18. Haven't you made a mistake in the account? Please receipt it.

19. What does one see yonder in the distance?

20. There you see a high mountain that commands a view of the whole country.

21. Where can we cross the river?

22. Take this road. At the village of B. there is a bridge.

6. Ich weisz hier nicht Bescheid. Ich suche die Wohnung des Bürgermeisters. Bin ich hier recht?

7. Nein! Sehen Sie nicht die Aufschrift (den Anschlag) "Eintritt Verboten" ("Kein Eingang")?

8. Wenden Sie sich nach links, bitte.

9. Ich möchte einige leichte Zigarren, etwas guten Tabak und drei Schachteln Zigaretten kaufen.

10. Diese sind sehr teuer. Haben Sie welche billigere?

11. Wie viel sagten Sie, dasz es mache?

12. Können Sie mir auf 10 Mark herausgeben? Nein, ich habe kein Geld bei mir.

13. Wo kann man Landkarten kaufen?

14. Beim Buchhändler um die Ecke.

15. Ich wünsche mit dem Wirt zu sprechen.

16. Sie müssen im voraus bezahlen. Ich musz darauf bestehen.

17. Was habe ich zu bezahlen?

18. Haben Sie sich nicht in der Rechnung geirrt? Ich bitte zu quittieren.

19. Was sieht man dort in der Ferne?

20. Da sehen Sie einen hohen Berg, der Aussicht über das ganze Land gewährt.

21. Wo kann man über den Flusz gehen?

22. Schlagen Sie diesen Weg ein. Beim Dorfe B. befindet sich eine Brücke.

23. How far from here?
24. About three kilometers (kilometer = approximately ⅝ mile.)
25. I must go to the city of M. This morning I missed the train. At what time does the next train leave?
26. The train is due.
27. How long do we stop in N.?
28. When do we reach there?
29. Is there a restaurant here?
30. What is ready? Bring me soup, roast beef and potatoes.
31. We have only ham, bread, eggs, cheese, sausage and beans. In this village you won't find anything else.
32. We wish to shelter eighteen soldiers.
33. This village must afford accommodations for a hundred men.
34. Water ⎫
     Feed   ⎬ our horses.
35. Fetch us milk, bread, meat, vegetables and coffee.

DRILL

1. Please tell me the name of this town. 2. As I am an entire stranger here, I should like to have a guide. (Führer, m.) 3. If you wish to get to the village N., take the third street to the right (rechts). 4. Ask this man if he could take us to N. 5. He says he does not

23. Wie weit von hier?
24. Ungefähr drei kilometer.
25. Ich musz nach der Stadt M. Heute morgen habe ich den Zug verpaszt. Um wie viel Uhr fährt der nächste Zug ab?
26. Der Zug ist fällig.
27. Wie lange Aufenthalt haben wir in N.?
28. Wann kommen wir dahin?
29. Gibt es hier ein Restaurant?
30. Was ist fertig? Bringen Sie mir Suppe, Rindfleisch und Kartoffeln.
31. Wir haben nur Schinken, Brot, Eier, Käse, Wurst und Bohnen. Anders finden Sie in diesem Dorfe nicht.
32. Wir wünschen achtzehn Soldaten zu unterbringen.
33. Dieses Dorf musz hundert Mann beherbergen.
34. Tränken } Sie unsere Pferde.
    Füttern
35. Holen Sie uns Milch, Brot, Fleisch, Gemüse und Kaffee.

Drill—(continued)

know the roads well. 6. Take me to the house of the Mayor. 7. He lives in (the) B. street. 8. Where can one buy tobacco? 9. These cigarettes are too expensive. Give me some cheaper [ones.]*

*Note: Words in square brackets are not to be translated.

IV

1. Is the health of the army good?

2. Epidemics have practically never occurred although the troops have often had to march through pest-ridden territory.

3. Thanks to hygienic measures the contagious diseases are continually decreasing.

4. A soldier receives perfect care in your army.

5. Yes. Read this report. 70% of the wounded become fit for service again.

6. R. is a member of the field ambulance service and was severely wounded last month by a shell. He was in the hospital three weeks.

7. Was an operation necessary?

8. Yes. His convalescence is now more rapid. They are granting him now two weeks more leave for recovery.

9. He will soon be sent back to his regiment.

10. How is Captain B.?

11. His complaint has grown worse. He is down with a fever. Also the shot has lamed his right arm.

12. You know his brother died last week. In the Battle of R. he was hit by a shell and he succumbed to his injuries.

13. I am very sorry to hear that. I had become acquainted with him at the university.

IV

1. Ist die Gesundheit des Heeres gut?
2. Epidemien sind fast gar nicht vorgekommen, obgleich die Truppen oft in verseuchtes Gebiet marschieren muszten.
3. Dank hygienischer Masznahmen nehmen die ansteckenden Krankheiten immer mehr ab.
4. Man hat bei Ihnen eine tadellose Verpflegung.
5. Ja. Lesen Sie diesen Bericht. Von den Verwundeten werden siebzig Prozent wieder dienstfähig.
6. R. ist Mitglied des Feldambulanzdienstes und wurde letzten Monat durch eine Granate schwer verwundet. Er lag drei Wochen im Lazarett.
7. Muszte eine Operation vorgenommen werden?
8. Ja. Nun geht seine Genesung schneller voran. Man gibt ihm jetzt noch zwei Wochen Erholungsurlaub.
9. Er wird wohl bald zu seinem Regiment geschickt werden.
10. Wie befindet sich Hauptmann B.?
11. Sein Leiden hat sich verschlimmert. Er liegt krank am Fieber. Auch hat ihm der Schusz den rechten Arm gelähmt.
12. Sein Bruder starb nämlich letzte Woche. In der Schlacht bei R. traf ihn eine Granate, und er ist seinen Verletzungen erlegen.
13. Es tut mir sehr leid das zu hören. Ich hatte ihn auf der Universität kennen gelernt.

14. Corporal N. is out of danger and will be discharged from the hospital next week.
15. During the winter many enemy troops died of pneumonia.
16. Is that a contagious disease?
17. Yes. It is caused by a germ.
18. It can be conveyed from one person to another by close contact. Everything ought to be disinfected.

DRILL

1. This prisoner tells me that the health of the German army is good. 2. I have read that epidemics have often occurred. 3. I believe the contagious diseases are decreasing. 4. In our army a soldier has always perfect care. 5. According to this report, eighty per cent of the wounded become fit for service again. 6. Ten of these soldiers are down with a fever. 7. How is that young captain who was severely wounded? He was in the hospital a month and they will probably grant him a month's leave for recovery. 8. Two prisoners have succumbed to their wounds. 9. Did many of your troops die of pneumonia? 10. In (bei) contagious diseases you must have everything disinfected.

14. Korporal N. ist auszer Gefahr und wird nächste Woche aus dem Lazarett entlassen werden.

15. Während des Winters sind viele feindliche Truppen an Lungenentzündung gestorben.

16. Ist die eine ansteckende Krankkeit?

17. Ja. Sie wird durch einen Keim verursacht.

18. Sie kann von einer Person auf eine andere bei naher Berührung übertragen werden. Man sollte alles desinfizieren lassen.

Diseases, Injuries, Etc.

Abscess, Eiterbeule, f.—n.
attack. Anfall, m. ⸚e.
bandage, *n.* Verband, m. ⸚e.
bleed, bluten.
blindness, Blindheit, f.
burn, Verbrennung, f. —en.
cholera, Cholera, f.
cold, catch —, sich erkälten.
constipation, Verstopfung, f.
consumption, Schwindsucht, f.
diarrhea, Durchfall, m.
diphtheria, Diphtheritis, f.
disinfect, desinfizieren.
dress a wound, einen Verband an-legen.
eruption, Ausschlag, m. ⸚e.
fatigue, Ermüdung. f. —.
fever, Fieber, n. —.

fracture, Bruch, m. ⸚e.
germ, Keim, m. —e.
hemorrhage, Blutung, f. —en.
infection, Ansteckung, f. —en.
inflammation, Entzündung, f. —en.
injury, Verletzung, f. —en.
medicine, Medizin, f. —en.
pain, Schmerz, m. —en.
plague, Pest, f.
pneumonia, Lungenentzündung, f.
poisoning, Vergiftung, f.
pus, Eiter, m.
small pox, Blattern (pl.).
sprain, *n.* Verrenkung, f. —en.
vomit, brechen.
wound, *n.* Wunde, f. —n.

V

1. The ambulance is bringing three wounded.
2. Where do you feel the pain?
3. My right arm hurts. I have violent pains.
4. We will probe the wound and put on a bandage.
5. I am not very well. I am hoarse and have a sore throat.
6. Draw a deep breath. This oil is for external use only.
7. How often during the day am I to take the medicine?
8. Three times a day. You have only caught cold. It will not be serious. Tomorrow you will be better.
9. You reported sick, didn't you?
10. Yes. I feel sick. The food does not agree with me.
11. You're only pretending to be sick.
12. For two days I have not been able to take any food. I have no appetite.
13. Well, I'll have the doctor summoned.
14. They are taking good care of you, aren't they?
15. O yes. Otherwise I feel very comfortable here. This little blanket however does not keep me warm. Might I have another?
16. I'll see to it.

V

1. Die Ambulanz bringt drei Verwundete.
2. Wo spüren Sie die Schmerzen?
3. Mir tut der rechte Arm weh. Ich habe heftige Schmerzen.
4. Wir wollen die Wunde sondieren und einen Verband anlegen.
5. Ich befinde mich nicht sehr wohl. Ich bin heiser und habe Halsweh.
6. Holen Sie tief Atem. Dieses Öl ist nur für äuszeren Gebrauch.
7. Wie oft des Tages soll ich die Medizin nehmen?
8. Dreimal des Tages. Sie haben sich nur erkältet. Es wird nicht von Bedeutung sein. Morgen befinden Sie sich schon besser.
9. Sie haben sich krank gemeldet, nicht wahr?
10. Ja. Mir ist übel. Die Speise bekommt mir nicht.
11. Sie stellen sich nur krank.
12. Seit zwei Tagen habe ich nichts zu mir nehmen können. Ich habe keinen Appetit.
13. Na! Ich lasse den Arzt holen.
14. Man pflegt Sie doch gut?
15. O Ja. Sonst ist mir ganz behaglich hier. Diese kleine Decke aber genügt mir nicht. Dürfte ich noch eine haben?
16. Ich will dafür sorgen.

VI

1. Come in!
2. You bade me come. At your service! What can I do for you?
3. I should like to ask you some questions.
4. Wait for me! I'll give you information. Follow me! Hurry up, won't you? Look here, will you?
5. Take it away! Get out of my way!
6. Be careful! Look out!
7. Don't ask so many questions!
8. Don't say anything for the present.
9. I wish to call your attention to the fact that you must write very explicitly.
10. Where are you from? Make your statement brief.
11. Mark that. Make a note of that.
12. Stop! Keep still! Not another word!
13. Get ready to go with me. The order is——
14. Get to work! Go to work!
15. Dress quickly! I'm in a hurry.
16. Well, going to be all day about it?
17. I am exhausted.
18. What's the meaning of that? What do you mean to say by that?
19. I am doing as much as ever I can.
20. Unfortunately I cannot change it.

VI

1. Herein!
2. Sie hieszen mich kommen. Zu Befehl! Was befehlen Sie?
3. Ich möchte Ihnen einige Fragen stellen.
4. Warten Sie auf mich! Ich sage Ihnen Bescheid. Folgen Sie mir! Machen Sie doch! Sehen Sie mal!
5. Weg damit! Gehen Sie mir aus dem Wege!
6. Vorsicht! Aufpassen!
7. So viel fragt man doch nicht!
8. Sagen Sie vorläufig nichts!
9. Ich will Sie darauf aufmerksam machen, dasz Sie recht ausführlich schreiben müssen.
10. Wo sind Sie her? Fassen Sie sich kurz!
11. Merken Sie das! Schreiben Sie das auf!
12. Hören Sie auf! Schweigen Sie! Kein Wort mehr!
13. Machen Sie sich fertig mitzugehen! Es heiszt hier——
14. Machen Sie sich an die Arbeit! Gehen Sie an die Arbeit.
15. Ziehen Sie sich schnell an! Ich habe Eile.
16. Na, wird's bald?
17. Ich kann nicht mehr.
18. Was soll das heiszen? Was wollen Sie damit sagen?
19. Ich tue so viel ich nur kann.
20. Leider kann ich es nicht ändern.

21. That may be hard, but you must try to get reconciled to it.
22. It serves you just right.
23. It is your fault. From now on things must go differently. It can't be helped.
24. I look upon it as my duty.
25. At all events you are to come tomorrow.
26. Just leave that to me.
27. I have finished with you. You may go. For further particulars apply to Officer N.
28. Official Announcement! At nine o'clock all lights must be extinguished.
29. We must search this building. Fetch me the keys at once.
30. You are to answer my questions.
31. Surrender! Lay down your arms!
32. You are wounded. We'll carry you to the field hospital. You'll get something to eat there too.

DRILL

1. Why don't you come in? 2. You must wait for me. 3. I shall ask you some questions and you are to (sollen) answer. 4. Tell me where you are from. 5. Write very explicitly. 6. Did I not say that you were to make your statement brief? 7. I'll make a note of that. 8. Are you ready to go with me or must I wait

21. Das mag schwer sein, aber Sie müssen sich darein finden.

22. Es geschieht Ihnen ganz recht.

23. Sie sind schuld daran. Von jetzt an musz es anders gehen. Es läszt sich nicht ändern.

24. Ich sehe es als meine Pflicht an.

25. Sie sollen auf jeden Fall morgen kommen.

26. Das werde ich schon machen.

27. Ich bin mit Ihnen fertig. Sie dürfen gehen. Wegen weiterer Erkundigungen wenden Sie sich an Offizier N.

28. Amtliche Bekanntmachung! Um neun Uhr müssen alle Lichter gelöscht werden.

29. Wir müssen dieses Gebäude untersuchen. Holen Sie mir sofort die Schlüssel.

30. Sie sollen auf meine Fragen antworten.

31. Ergebt euch! Streckt die Waffen!

32. Sie sind verwundet. Wir tragen Sie in das Feldlazarett. Sie sollen dort auch zu essen bekommen.

Drill—(continued)

for you? Hurry up, won't you? 9. The order is to go to work at half past six. 10. That I cannot change. These prisoners must dress quickly and get to work. 11. It's their fault and it serves them right.

VII

1. What is your name?
2. My name is N. The other man is a lieutenant by the name of Bauer. He is short of stature.
3. That's immaterial. Please tell me to what regiment you belong.
4. Say it again.
5. How old are you? Do you know German?
6. Give me an English-German dictionary. What is —— in German? We'll look it up.
7. Is there anyone here who speaks English? I know only a little German.
8. I find it difficult to express myself correctly in German.
9. Where are you from? You are from Berlin, aren't you? And where did you report for service?
10. Where did you get that?
11. I got that as a present.
12. What am I to infer from that?
13. You may not keep that.
14. Translate this letter. Did you understand me?
15. Correct (that agrees). There, that will do. I must confiscate it.
16. How does it happen that ——?
17. He claims to have seen it himself.
18. We went in the direction of the village.

VII

1. Wie heiszen Sie?
2. Ich heisze N. Der andere ist ein Leutnant namens Bauer. Er ist kurz von Figur.
3. Das tut nichts zur Sache. Sagen Sie mir nur, welchem Regiment Sie angehören.
4. Sagen Sie es noch einmal.
5. Wie alt sind Sie? Können Sie Deutsch?
6. Geben Sie mir ein englisch-deutsches Wörterbuch. Wie heiszt —— auf Deutsch? Wir wollen nachschlagen.
7. Ist jemand hier, der Englisch spricht? Ich kann nur ein bischen Deutsch.
8. Ich finde es schwer, mich deutsch richtig auszudrücken.
9. Wo sind Sie her? Sie sind ein Berliner, nicht wahr? Und Ihre Meldungsstelle?
10. Wo haben Sie das her?
11. Das habe ich geschenkt bekommen.
12. Was soll man daraus schlieszen?
13. Das dürfen Sie nicht behalten.
14. Übersetzen Sie diesen Brief. Haben Sie mich verstanden?
15. Das stimmt. So, jetzt ist's genug! Ich musz es konfiszieren.
16. Wie kommt es, dasz ——?
17. Er will es selbst gesehen haben.
18. Wir gingen nach dem Dorfe zu.

19. Stick to the point.
20. That is pure invention. The case is just the reverse. The facts of the case are these.
21. I take it seriously.
22. I am quite exhausted.
23. You will be well cared for. Drink this hot soup.
24. Here is a warm blanket and a woolen muffler for you.
25. You have enough as it is.
26. I feel quite comfortable here.
27. You are well off.
28. If that is all, you may go.

DRILL

1. What is the name of this wounded [man]? 2. To what regiment does he belong? 3. Look up this word in the dictionary. 4. Can't you express yourself correctly in English? 5. Tell me where you reported for service. 6. May I not keep this little book? I got it as a present from my mother. 7. Yes, but the other things (Sache f.) will be confiscated. 8. This man is quite exhausted. Could you give him something to eat? 9. Here is some hot soup. 10. There, now you are quite comfortable.

19. Bleiben Sie bei der Sache.
20. Das ist rein aus der Luft gegriffen. Der Fall ist gerade umgekehrt. Die Sache verhält sich so.
21. Ich nehme es für Ernst auf.
22. Ich kann nicht mehr.
23. Man wird Sie gut pflegen. Trinken Sie diese heisze Suppe.
24. Hier haben Sie eine warme Decke und ein wollenes Halstuch.
25. Sie haben so schon genug.
26. Mir ist es ganz behaglich hier.
27. Sie haben es gut.
28. Wenn's weiter nichts ist, so dürfen Sie gehen.

Additional Notes

VIII

1. For whom are you looking? What do you want?
2. Have you writing paper and ink?
3. These prisoners give me a great deal of trouble. Don't interrupt me.
4. These books are at your disposal.
5. You must put up with it.
6. Very well. (All right.)
7. How are things going?
8. What is there new?
9. Nothing that I know of.
10. You can't believe him.
11. There is something under way.
12. You can depend on it.
13. When is the new offensive to begin?
14. The first of next month. (Toward the middle of June. In the course of a week.)
15. That sounds well. Just go on.
16. I grant that he is right.
17. Where can we find that out?
18. The disease is spreading. Many troops are affected.
19. They are very badly off.
20. Have you a certificate of vaccination?
21. What does this soldier speak of in the diary that you found?
22. I'll read some passages to you:—

"Brave defence in the fight at ·N. On the first of August fresh forces are to arrive. We shall then employ large numbers of machine guns."

VIII

1. Zu wem wollen Sie? Was wünschen Sie?
2. Haben Sie Schreibpapier und Tinte?
3. Diese Gefangenen machen mir viel zu schaffen. Unterbrechen Sie mich nicht!
4. Diese Bücher stehen Ihnen zur Verfügung.
5. Sie müssen sich damit zufrieden geben.
6. Schon gut!
7. Wie wird es?
8. Was gibt's Neues?
9. Nichts, das ich wüszte.
10. Man kann ihm nicht glauben.
11. Es ist etwas im Werke.
12. Sie können darauf rechnen.
13. Wann soll die neue Offensive anfangen?
14. Den ersten künftigen Monats. (Gegen Mitte Juni. Im Laufe von acht Tagen.)
15. Das läszt sich hören. Fahren Sie nur fort.
16. Ich gebe ihm recht.
17. Wo können wir das ausfindig machen?
18. Die Krankheit greift um sich. Viele Truppen sind behaftet.
19. Es geht ihnen recht schlecht.
20. Haben Sie einen Impfschein?
21. Wovon spricht dieser Soldat in dem Tagebuch, das Sie gefunden haben?
22. Ich lese Ihnen einige Stellen vor:—

"Wackere Verteidigung im Kampf bei N. Am ersten August sollen frische Streitkräfte eintreffen. Wir werden dann grosze Mengen Maschinengewehre anwenden."

IX

1. These soldiers are now on leave. Day after tomorrow they are going into the trenches again.

2. I think as a rule people have a false idea about life in the trenches. The life is not as the "movies" represent it.

3. What did that prisoner of war tell you?

4. He said that the famous General D. would personally lead their new offensive.

5. For five days he has been staying at this front, in a continual endeavor to put fire into the soldiers.

6. I believe that a new offensive is impending.

7. South of N. the enemy succeeded by means of bringing up superior forces in driving back a part of our front. This is not however a key position of any importance.

8. What does the army headquarters report today?

9. It reports that the troops have conquered several sections of enemy trenches.

10. How do things stand on the northern theater of war?

11. There we have gained a strategic advantage.

12. Sixteen enemy divisions attacked our positions there. In counter attacks these were regained: 600 prisoners, among them twelve officers, also eight machine guns fell into our possession.

IX

1. Diese Soldaten haben jetzt Urlaub. Übermorgen gehen sie wieder in die Schützengräben.
2. Ich glaube, man macht sich allgemein eine falsche Vorstellung über das Leben in den Schützengräben. Das Leben ist nicht, wie es Kinos repräsentieren.
3. Was hat Ihnen der Kriegsgefangene erzählt?
4. Er sagte, dasz der berühmte General D. die neue Offensive persönlich anführen werde.
5. Seit fünf Tagen weilt er an dieser Front, unablässig bestrebt, die Soldaten anzufeuern.
6. Ich glaube, dasz eine neue Offensive bevorsteht.
7. Südlich von N. ist es dem Feinde gelungen unter Ansetzung überlegener Kräfte einen Teil unserer Fronte zurückzudrängen. Das ist aber keine Schlüsselstellung von Bedeutung.
8. Was berichtet die Heeresleitung heute?
9. Sie berichtet, dasz die Truppen mehrere Teile feindlicher Schützengräben erobert haben.
10. Wie steht es auf dem nördlichen Kriegsschauplatz?
11. Da haben wir einen strategischen Vorteil errungen.
12. Sechzehn feindliche Divisionen griffen unsere dortigen Stellungen an. In Gegenangriffen wurden dieselben zurückerobert: sechs hundert Gefangene, darunter zwölf Offiziere, sowie acht Maschinengewehre sind in unsere Hände gefallen.

13. In the sector between A. and B unusually violent artillery battles continue.

14. After penetrating our line at a few points the enemy troops were repulsed everywhere by our regiments in hand-to-hand fighting.

15. In these engagements we took many captives.

16. The enemy has captured the town of M. with the greatest sacrifices. The headquarters announces more than 500 captives but insignificant booty.

17. In three places these troops made successful drives yesterday.

18. The batteries have been bombarding hostile positions and three provision columns along the northern slopes of the mountain were dispersed.

19. Yesterday's report about the air attack upon the city of B. announces that all the airmen returned without loss.

20. Today's papers however contradict this report and add that one airplane was brought down.

DRILL

1. How long are you on leave? 2. Next week we have to go into the trenches again. 3. You have a false idea about the life in the trenches. 4. Why is General D. staying at this front? 5. Those prisoners told me yes-

13. Im Abschnitt zwischen A. und B. dauern auszerordentlich heftige Artilleriekämpfe an.

14. An wenigen Punkten in unsere Linie eingedrungen, sind die feindlichen Truppen von unseren Regimentern überall im Handgemenge zurückgeworfen worden.

15. In diesen Kämpfen haben wir viele Gefangene gemacht.

16. Der Feind hat die Stadt M. unter schwersten Opfern genommen. Die Heeresleitung meldet mehr als 500 Gefangene aber geringe Beute.

17. An drei Stellen haben diese Truppen gestern erfolgreiche Vorstösze unternommen.

18. Die Batterien haben feindliche Stellungen beschossen und drei Proviantkolonnen an den nördlichen Abhängen des Berges wurden zerstreut.

19. Der gestrige amtliche Bericht über den Luftangriff auf die Stadt B. meldet, dasz alle Flieger ohne Verlust zurückgekehrt sind.

20. Die heutigen Zeitungen aber widersprechen diesem Bericht, und fügen hinzu, dasz ein Flugzeug heruntergeholt worden sei.

Drill—(continued)

terday that he is going to lead the new offensive. 6. Does General D. believe that he can drive back our front? 7. He thinks this is a key position of great importance.

X

1. Official announcement is made [of the following]:

West of D. a further position of the enemy was stormed. Successful mine explosions injured the enemy's position at N.

2. Counter attacks failed. Our airmen bombarded the city of L.

3. The enemy evacuated yesterday the right bank of the river. Otherwise the situation in the northeast remains unchanged with no especial occurrences.

4. A soldier has intercepted a telegram that contains something interesting. Can you translate it? Read it to me.

5. Storming party is in readiness for the attack intended. We resume offensive tomorrow and support attack by artillery.

6. Day after tomorrow we intend to cross the river at B. We are having the bridge at R. blown up tonight.

7. Take possession of the heights southwest of R. At the border the positions remain entirely in our possession.

8. After a short fight a foothold was obtained on the northern bank. When the enemy offered resistance they were driven back by powerful attacks.

X

1. Amtlich wird gemeldet:
Westlich von D. wurde eine weitere Stellung des Feindes gestürmt. Erfolgreiche Minensprengungen beschädigten die feindliche Stellung bei N.

2. Gegenangriffe scheiterten. Unsere Flieger haben die Stadt L. mit Bomben beworfen.

3. Der Feind räumte gestern das rechte Ufer des Flusses. Sonst im Nordosten bei unveränderter Lage keine besonderen Ereignisse.

4. Ein Soldat hat ein Telegramm aufgefangen, das etwas Interessantes enthält. Können Sie es übersetzen? Lesen Sie es mir vor.

5. Für den beabsichtigten Angriff sind die Sturmtruppen bereit gestellt. Wir nehmen morgen die Offensive wieder auf und unterstützen den Angriff durch Artillerie.

6. Übermorgen beabsichtigen wir den Flusz bei B. zu überschreiten. Wir lassen heute nacht die Brücke bei R. sprengen.

7. Bemächtigt euch der Höhen südwestlich von R. An der Grenze bleiben die Stellungen vollständig in unserem Besitze.

8. Nach kurzem Kampf wurde auf dem nördlichen Ufer Fusz gefaszt. Wo der Feind Widerstand leistete, wurde er durch kräftige Angriffe zurückgetrieben.

9. In consequence of our forward movement they gave up their positions west of the river.

10. The headquarters announces this evening the capture of the capital.

DRILL

1 What is the official announcement? 2. Did those mine explosions injure your positions? 3. It is officially announced that the city of L. is being bombarded. 4. Why did your troops evacuate that position? 5. Our storming party was in readiness but the attack failed. 6. The enemy intended to cross the river but the bridge had already been blown up. 7. Are the positions at the border in your possession? 8. You offered resistance, but were driven back by our powerful attacks. 9. Yes, we had to give up the positions west of the river.

9. Infolge unserer Vorwärtsbewegung haben sie ihre Stellungen westlich des Flusses aufgegeben.

10. Die Heeresleitung meldet heute abend die Einnahme von der Hauptstadt.

Additional Notes

XI
ATTACK ON FORTIFIED CITY.

1. The city of M is a very strong fortress and is soon to be attacked by our troops.
2. The bridge head at N fell into our hands yesterday.
3. The siege of the city will probably last several weeks.
4. The pioneers have restored the railroad bridge destroyed by the enemy.
5. Yesterday an armored train attacked Fort B of the outer line of fortifications.
6. A second fort of the outer ring was carried by storm by the infantry.
7. The garrison put up a brave defense but was not equal to the strong attack.
8. A division of marines participated in the attack.
9. Two more forts and the redoubts lying between them have fallen.
10. In this operation twenty cannon were taken.
11. This gap made in the outer circle of fortifications opens the way to an attack on the inner line of forts.
12. The inner forts of D and E were silenced today.
13. We have just made announcement of our intention of bombarding the city.

XI

1. Die Stadt M ist eine sehr starke Festung and wird bald von unseren Truppen angegriffen.
2. Gestern fiel der Brückenkopf bei N in unsere Hände.
3. Die Belagerung der Stadt wird wohl mehrere Wochen dauern.
4. Die Eisenbahner haben die vom Feinde zerstörte Eisenbahnbrücke wiederhergestellt.
5. Gestern griff ein Panzerzug das Fort B der äuszeren Linie an.
6. Ein zweites Fort des äuszeren Gürtels wurde von der Infanterie erstürmt.
7. Die Besatzung hat sich tapfer verteidigt aber sie war dem starken Angriff nicht gewachsen.
8. Eine Marine-Division hat sich an dem Sturm beteiligt.
9. Noch zwei Forts und die dazwischen liegenden Redouten sind gefallen.
10. In diesem Gefecht wurden zwanzig Geschütze erobert.
11. Diese in den äuszeren Fortgürtel gebrochene Lücke gestattet den Angriff gegen die innere Fortslinie vorzutragen.
12. Die inneren Forts D und E wurden heute zum Schweigen gebracht.
13. Wir haben soeben die Beschieszung der Stadt angekündigt.

14. The commander has declared his willingness to accept responsibility for the bombardment.
15. The bombardment was exceedingly violent.
16. After a few hours a white flag appeared on the citadel.
17. Firing was stopped last evening at half past seven at the command of the general.
18. The negotiations for the surrender were at once begun with the commander.
19. The city has been obliged to surrender unconditionally.
20. Our troops held a triumphant entry into the city this morning.
21. One of the strongest fortresses in the whole country has thus finally come into our possession.
22. The number of prisoners cannot yet be determined and the booty is very great.

DRILL

1. Our troops are attacking a strong fortress. 2. The city will soon fall into our hands. 3. An armored train is attacking the outer line of fortifications. 4. The garrison was not equal to the strong attack. 5. The enemy announces his intention of bombarding the city. 6. Many cannon have been taken and two more forts silenced. 7. The negotiations for surrender will be begun at

14. Der Kommandant hat erklärt, die Verantwortung für die Beschieszung der Stadt übernehmen zu wollen.
15. Die Beschieszung war äuszerst heftig.
16. Nach einigen Stunden erschien eine weisze Fahne auf der Citadelle.
17. Gestern abend um halb acht auf Befehl des Generals wurde das Feuer eingestellt.
18. Die Übergabeverhandlungen mit dem Kommandanten wurden sofort begonnen.
19. Die Stadt hat sich auf Gnade und Ungnade ergeben müssen.
20. Unsere Truppen hielten heute morgen ihren siegreichen Einzug in die Stadt.
21. Eine der stärksten Festungen des ganzen Landes ist also endlich in unserem Besitz.
22. Die Zahl der Gefangenen läszt sich noch nicht übersehen, und die Beute ist sehr grosz.

Drill—(continued)

once. 8. They must surrender unconditionally. 9. Which is the strongest fortress in the whole country? 10. They have not yet determined the number of prisoners.

XII
UNIFORMS—WEAPONS—BILLETS

1. The uniform is a military necessity for a soldier to make clear his membership in the army and in a definite branch of the service.
2. In war times only the uniform gives one the right to bear arms.
3. In times of peace military men often wear bright colored uniforms especially when on parade.
4. In war times the officer as well as the private wears simple, gray clothing.
5. In the trenches one has to wear a steel helmet for protection against shell fragments.
6. In the rest camps however the comfortable round cloth cap is worn.
7. The usual spiked, leather helmet or "Pickelhaube" is out of fashion at the front.
8. Bright brass buttons have also been banished as dangerous.
9. During bad weather boots and warm overcoats are necessary.
10. Regimental insignia are worn on the shoulder straps.
11. The soldier has to carry his pack with him on the march.
12. This consists of his knapsack, his mess kit and his folded overcoat.
13. Besides this the infantryman must carry his rifle, side arms and ammunition belt.

XII

1. Die Uniform des Soldaten ist kriegsrechtlich notwendig, um die Zugehörigkeit zum Heere und zu einem bestimmten Truppenkörper kenntlich zu machen.

2. Im Kriege berechtigt erst die Uniform zum Waffengebrauch.

3. Im Frieden trägt der Militär oft eine bunte Uniform, besonders auf Parade.

4. Im Kriege trägt der Offizier sowohl wie der gemeine Soldat einfache, graue Bekleidung.

5. In den Schützengräben musz man zum Schutz gegen Granatsplitter einen Stahlhelm aufsetzen.

6. In den Ruhelagern aber wird die bequeme, runde Tuchmütze getragen.

7. Der übliche Lederhelm oder Pickelhaube ist auszer Mode an der Front.

8. Blanke Messingknöpfe sind auch verbannt als etwas Gefährliches.

9. Beim schlechten Wetter sind hohe Stiefel und warme Überzieher notwendig.

10. Regimentsabzeichen werden an den Achselklappen getragen.

11. Der Soldat musz sein Gepäck auf dem Marsch mitnehmen.

12. Dies besteht aus dem Tornister, dem Kochgeschirr und dem zusammengerollten Mantel.

13. Auszerdem musz der Infanterist sein Gewehr, Seitengewehr, sowie die Patrontasche tragen.

14. The cavalry man rides on horseback and has a sabre and a lance.

15. In the present war it has become necessary to have gas masks constantly at hand.

16. Behind the front trenches dugouts have been built in which the troops live.

17. After service at the front the men are withdrawn to villages farther back where they are billeted in the village houses.

18. Here they are permitted to rest up for a longer or shorter period.

19. The army postal service brings them many letters and packages from home.

20. After a period of rest the soldiers must again resume work.

DRILL

1. Why does a soldier wear a uniform? 2. To what branch of the service does he belong? 3. When we have peace, the military often wear gay uniforms. 4. In war times only plain uniforms are worn. 5. Shiny brass buttons and bright colors are a dangerous thing. 6. Have you your knapsack and

14. Der berittene Soldat reitet mit Säbel und Lanze versehen.

15. In dem jetzigen Kriege ist es notwendig geworden, Gasmasken beständig bei sich zu haben.

16. Hinter den vordersten Schützengräben sind Unterstände gebaut worden, worin die Mannschaften wohnen.

17. Nach dem Frontdienst werden die Mannschaften nach weiter zurückgelegenen Dörfern zurückgezogen und erhalten Quartier in den Dorfhäusern.

18. Hier dürfen sie sich auf längere Zeit ausruhen.

19. Die Feldpost bringt ihnen viele Briefe und Pakete.

20. Nach einer Ruhepause müssen die Soldaten wieder antreten.

Drill—(continued)

mess kit with you? 7. Come into the dugout. We must get our gas masks. 8. To-morrow we are going back to some remote villages, where we can rest. 9. I hope I shall get some letters and packages. 10. After about two weeks we shall be obliged to resume work again.

XIII

AIRPLANES AND AIRSHIPS

1. Flying craft are of the greatest importance in up-to-date reconnaissance and fighting.
2. In former wars balloons were used for reconnaissance work but nowadays captive balloons, airships and airplanes are all three used for this work.
3. The two latter are also used for fighting purposes.
4. Captive balloons behind the lines observe the effect of artillery fire and assist in its direction.
5. Dirigible airships, so-called Zeppelins, are useful for reconnoitring and in some measure for fighting but their relatively low speed limits their usefulness.
6. The chief advantages of the airplane lie in its small size and in its speed.
7. They often fly at a speed of more than seventy-five miles an hour and at very great heights.
8. The pilot and the observer have a broad view and in consequence of the distance from the ground their observations are not interfered with by the speed.
9. The motor is the soul of the machine and upon its smooth running depends the success of the flight.

XIII

1. Das Flugzeug ist von gröszter Bedeutung in dem modernsten Erkundungs-und Kampfwesen.

2. In früheren Kriegen wurde der Luftballon in dem Erkundungsdienst gebraucht, aber heutzutage hat man den Fesselballon, das lenkbare Luftschiff und das Flugzeug zu diesem Zweck.

3. Die beiden letzteren werden auch zu Kampfzwecken gebraucht.

4. Fesselballone hinter den Frontlinien beobachten den Erfolg des Artilleriefeuers und nehmen Teil an der Verteilung davon.

5. Die lenkbaren Luftschiffe, auch Zeppelins genannt, sind für Aufklärungstätigkeit und gewissermaszen für den Kampf brauchbar, aber ihre verhältnismäszig niedrige Geschwindigkeit beschränkt ihre Brauchbarkeit.

6. Die Hauptvorteile des Flugzeugs liegen in seiner Kleinheit und Geschwindigkeit.

7. Sie fliegen sehr oft mit einer Geschwindigkeit von mehr als hundert Kilometer pro Stunde und in sehr groszer Höhe.

8. Führer und Beobachter haben einen weiten Ausblick, und infolge der Entfernung vom Erdboden werden ihre Beobachtungen durch die Geschwindigkeit nicht mehr beinträchtigt.

9. Der Motor ist die Seele des Flugzeugs, und von seinem guten Lauf hängt das Gelingen des Flugs ab.

10. If the motor stops the pilot must resort to gliding.

11. Some machines are provided with bombs which are usually dropped upon hostile hangars, railroads, etc.

12. They also carry machine guns with which they try to shoot down hostile machines or to attack marching troops.

13. The airman is always in danger of being attacked from the ground as well as from the air.

14. Special cannon, called anti-aircraft cannon, are used to shoot down hostile planes.

15. In any case the life of an airman is full of danger and he must undergo a long and arduous training before he is prepared for this branch of the service.

DRILL

1. Can you see that captive balloon up there?
2. What are the chief advantages of an airplane?
3. They fly at great speed and are quite small.
4. If the motor stops, what does the pilot have to do?
5. What sort of guns do flying craft carry? 6. Did

10. Bleibt der Motor stehen, so musz der Führer zum Gleitflug übergehen.

11. Einige Flugzeuge werden mit Fallbomben ausgerüstet, welche gewöhnlich auf feindliche Luftschiffhallen, Eisenbahnen usw. abgeworfen werden.

12. Sie tragen auch Maschinengewehre, womit man versucht Flugzeuge des Feindes abzuschieszen oder marschierende Truppen anzugreifen.

13. Der Flieger ist stets in Gefahr vom Erdboden aus so wie von der Luft angegriffen zu werden.

14. Besondere Geschütze, die sogenannten Ballonkanonen, werden gebraucht um feindliche Flugzeuge abzuschieszen.

15. Jedenfalls ist das Leben des Fliegers sehr gefährlich und er musz eine lange, mühsame Ausbildung durchmachen, ehe er bereit ist diesen Dienst aufzunehmen.

Drill—(continued)

you ever see a dirigible balloon or a Zeppelin? 7. Upon what does the success of the flight all depend? 8. The enemy have dropped bombs on our hangars. 9. The airman was attacked by anti-aircraft cannon. 10. When shall you be prepared to enter this branch of the service?

XIV

NAVY

1. The fleet is going to put to sea to-day.

2. Four battleships and the appropriate cruisers and torpedoboats are on a practice cruise.

3. Admiral B. is on board the flagship.

4. The whole navy is especially proud of the new fast cruiser H which has only been in service two weeks.

5. The whole prescribed equipment has in the meantime been brought on board by the new crew.

6. The ship has a length of 600 feet, 95 foot beam, and draws 26 feet. Her displacement is 23,000 and she can develop 52,000 horsepower and a speed of 28 knots.

7. She is an armored cruiser and carries ten 10 inch, twelve 6 inch and twelve 3 inch guns together with two machine guns and four torpedo tubes.

8. Her crew consists of 1,050 men including officers and engineers.

9. The whole fleet is going to take part in manoeuvers and target practice.

10. In the evening all the ships are to return to the harbor.

XIV

1. Die Flotte geht heute in die See.
2. Vier Linienschiffe und die entsprechenden Kreuzer und Torpedoboote machen eine Übungsfahrt.
3. Der Groszadmiral B. ist an Bord des Flottenflaggschiffs.
4. Die ganze Marine ist ganz besonders stolz auf den groszen Kreuzer H., dessen Indienststellung erst vor vierzehn Tagen stattfand.
5. Die ganze vorgeschriebene Ausrüstung ist inzwischen von der neuen Besatzung an Bord gebracht worden.
6. Der Kreuzer hat 186 m. (Meter) Länge, 30 m. Breite und 8.2 m. Tiefgang. Die Wasserverdrängung ist 23,000 und das Schiff kann 52,000 Pferdekräfte und eine Geschwindigkeit von 28 Knoten entwickeln.
7. Es ist ein Panzerkreuzer und trägt als Armierung zehn 28 cm., zwölf 15 cm. und zwölf 8.8 cm. Geschütze, sowie zwei Maschinengewehre und vier Torpedoröhre.
8. Die Besatzung besteht aus 1,050 Mann einschlieszlich Offiziere und Ingenieurs.
9. Die ganze Flotte wird an Fahrtübungen und an Schieszübung teilnehmen.
10. Am Abend sollen alle Schiffe wieder in den Hafen einlaufen.

11. The commander of the ship is Captain C. He is standing up there on the bridge on the starboard side.

12. The sailors are cleaning ship under the direction of the chief mate.

13. After the fleet has reached the shooting grounds a tug with a large target will be ready to start at a given signal.

14. The guns are loaded and the distance set off on the sights. The commander gives the order, "Open fire," which is sent by an officer to the guns.

15. The eyes of all are directed at the target.

16. High columns of water mixed with powder smoke and shell fragments rise behind the target.

17. Some shots seem to have landed home.

18. After some time comes the command, "Cease fire." The hits are counted and the target brought on board.

19. The admiral discusses the shooting and praises the ability of the crew.

20. Eight bells sounds and the boatswain's mates pipe for dinner.

DRILL

1. How many battleships are there in the fleet? 2. I think I see an armored cruiser and two torpedo boats. 3. Why is the crew proud of their new ship? 4. What is the fleet going to do?

11. Der Kommandant des Schiffes ist Kapitän zur See C. Er steht oben auf der Kommandobrücke an der Steuerbordseite.

12. Die Matrosen reinigen das Schiff unter der Aufsicht des Obermaats.

13. Nachdem die Flotte den Schieszplatz erreicht hat, wird ein Schleppdampfer mit einer groszen Scheibe bereit liegen, um auf Signal anzulaufen.

14. Die Geschütze sind schon geladen und die Entfernung an den Aufsätzen der Geschütze eingestellt. Der Kommandant gibt den Befehl, "Feuer eröffnen," der von einem Offiziere an die Geschütze weitergegeben wird.

15. Aller Augen werden auf die Scheibe gerichtet.

16. Hohe Wassersäulen mit Pulverrauch und Sprengstücken vermischt steigen hinter der Scheibe auf.

17. Einige Geschosse scheinen gut getroffen zu haben.

18. Nach einiger Zeit heiszt es, "Batterie halt." Die Volltreffer werden gezählt, und das Scheibenbild an Bord gebracht.

19. Der Admiral bespricht das Schieszen und lobt die Tüchtigkeit der Mannschaft.

20. Die Schiffsglocke schlägt acht Glas, und die Bootsmannsmaate pfeifen "Alle Mann mittag."

XV
FIRING DATA

1. The battery will take up its position behind that hill, where it will be concealed by the trees.
2. The target is the enemy's trenches near yonder city.
3. The battery commander (B. C.) is on that hill two hundred yards directly to the left of the battery.
4. He has his B.C. telescope and range finder with him.
5. Several officers assist him in his observations.
6. The target is not visible from the guns.
7. The aiming point, which is visible at the guns, is a church steeple 4,000 yards to the rear.
8. The range finder shows that the target is 3,000 yards distant.
9. The deflection at the B.C. station is estimated at 2,500 mils.
10. The B.C. station is twenty yards above the guns and twelve yards above the target, so that the site (guns to target) is 305.
11. The angle of departure for 3,000 yards is 90 mils.
12. The parallax of the aiming point is five mils.
13. The deflection difference for the initial command will be +10 (open ten mils).

XV

1. Die Batterie nimmt Stellung hinter jenem Hügel, wo sie durch die Bäume verborgen wird.
2. Das Ziel ist die Schützengräben des Feindes in der Nähe von jener Stadt.
3. Der Batteriechef befindet sich auf jener Höhe 180 m. gerade links von der Batterie.
4. Er hat das Batteriefernrohr (oder Scherenfernrohr) und den Entfernungsmesser mit sich.
5. Verschiedene Offiziere sind ihm bei den Beobachtungen behilflich.
6. Das Ziel ist von der Batterie aus nicht sichtbar.
7. Der von den Geschützen sichtbare Zielpunkt ist jener 3,600 m. nach hinten liegende Kirchturm.
8. Der Entfernungsmesser zeigt, dasz das Ziel 2,700 m. entfernt ist.
9. Die Abweichung bei dem Batteriechefsposten wird auf 2,500 geschätzt.
10. Der Batteriechefsposten ist 18 m. über den Geschützen und 8.4 m. über dem Ziel. Also ist der Erhöhungswinkel 305.
11. Der Abgangswinkel für 2,700 m. beträgt 90 mils.
12. Die Parallaxe des Zielpunkts beträgt fünf mils.
13. Der Seitenverschiebungsunterschied für den ersten Befehl wird +10 (10 mehr) sein.

14. To clear the crest the minimum range must be 2,500 yards.
15. The corrector for the day is 31 and a height of burst of two mils is desired.
16. After the initial salvo two shots are observed to be over and two short.
17. Thirty per cent of the shots burst on graze.
18. An aviator is to report on the results of the firing.
19. After fifteen minutes' shooting the target is reported demolished.
20. This is a good result for indirect firing.

DRILL

1. Where has the battery taken up its position? 2. The battery commander will stand on that hill and announce the target and aiming-point. 3. Who will assist him? 4. The range-finder and battery commander's telescope have been brought along. 5. The range (Tragweite), the deflection and the site have been found. 6. What is the angle of departure for 2,500 yards? 7. When will the target be destroyed? 8. What percentage of the shots burst on graze? 9. How many shots were short and how many over? 10. What success did you have?

14. Um die Krete abzukämmen musz das minimum Visier 2,250 m. sein.

15. Der normale Schieber für heute ist 31, und eine Sprenghöhe von zwei wird erwünscht.

16. Nach dem ersten Gang erscheinen zwei Geschosse kurz und zwei weit.

17. Dreiszig Prozent der Geschosze sprengen beim Aufprall.

18. Ein Flieger soll das Resultat der Beschieszung melden.

19. Nach einer Viertelstunde berichtet man, dasz das Ziel zerstört ist.

20. Dies ist ein guter Erfolg für indirektes Schieszen.

Additional Notes

XVI

Merchant Marine—Blockade—Submarine

1. The enemy has declared a blockade of the whole coast.
2. All steamers, sailing vessels, etc. are being stopped and searched.
3. If they contain contraband of war, they must put about and undergo a careful search in the enemy's harbors.
4. Even neutral ships form no exception to this rule.
5. All forbidden cargoes and often the ships also are confiscated.
6. Yesterday several fishing vessels were stopped, searched and sunk with bombs.
7. The captains and their crews were allowed to go in their small boats.
8. A large schooner loaded with cotton and another carrying grain and a deck load of lumber were set on fire and destroyed.
9. The largest mail and passenger steamers are often able to escape the blockade through their speed.
10. International law allows hospital ships under the protection of the Red Cross free passage.
11. Submarines have contributed much in the execution of this blockade.

XVI

1. Der Feind hat die ganze Küste in Blockadezustand erklärt.
2. Sämtliche Dampfer, Segelschiffe usw. werden angehalten und untersucht.
3. Wenn sie Konterbande enthalten, so müssen sie umkehren und in den Häfen des Feindes sorgsam untersucht werden.
4. Selbst neutrale Fahrzeuge bilden keine Ausnahme.
5. Sämtliche verbotene Ladungen und manchmal auch die Dampfer selber werden eingezogen.
6. Gestern wurden mehrere Fischerboote aufgehalten, untersucht und durch Bomben versenkt.
7. Die Kapitäne und die Mannschaften durften in Ruderbooten entkommen.
8. Ein groszer Schoner mit Baumwolle und noch einer mit Getreide und einer Deckladung Bauholz wurden in Brand gesteckt und zerstört.
9. Die gröszten Post- und Passagierdampfer können oft durch ihre grosze Schnelligkeit der Blockade entgehen.
10. Das Völkerrecht erlaubt Krankenschiffen unter dem Schutz des Roten Kreuzes freien Durchgang.
11. Unterseeboote haben viel beigetragen diese Blockade durchzuführen.

12. The larger and newer submarines or U-boats, as they are called, are often 300 feet long.

13. Many of them can cruise thousands of miles and have a speed of about twenty knots.

14. Their real weapon is the torpedo but most of them are also equipped with light deck guns.

15. When the weather is good they cruise on the surface, if no enemy is near.

16. Petroleum motors furnish the driving force when not submerged, but storage batteries furnish the electric force for under water sailing.

17. When under water it is possible to observe the surface of the ocean through the periscope.

18. When a hostile ship appears a torpedo is fired through the torpedo tube.

19. Through the explosion of the missile the ship is sunk.

20. Submarines have caused great damage to merchant shipping, but war vessels have suffered only relatively small loss.

DRILL

1. We shall declare a blockade of the whole coast and stop all steamers and sailing vessels. 2. All vessels must be searched. 3. We have sometimes confiscated the cargoes of even neutral ships. 4. Mail and passenger steamers have great speed and often escape. 5. International law

12. Die größeren und neueren Unterseeboote oder U-Boote, wie man sie auch nennt, haben oft 300 Fusz Länge.

13. Manche davon können Tausende von Meilen fahren und haben eine Geschwindigkeit von ungefähr zwanzig Knoten.

14. Ihre eigentliche Waffe ist der Torpedo, aber die meisten sind auch mit leichten Deckgeschützen versehen.

15. Wenn das Wetter gut ist, fahren sie auf der Oberfläche des Meeres, wenn kein Feind in der Nähe ist.

16 Aufgetaucht liefern Petroleummotoren die Triebkraft, aber die Akkumulatorenbatterie liefert die elektrische Kraft für die Unterwasserfahrt.

17. Unter Wasser ist es möglich die Oberfläche des Meeres durch das Periskop zu beobachten.

18. Wenn ein feindliches Schiff erscheint, wird ein Torpedo durch das Torpedorohr lanciert.

19. Durch das Explodieren (Sprengen) des Geschosses wird das Schiff zum Sinken gebracht.

20. Die Unterseeboote haben der Handelsmarine groszen Schaden beigebracht, aber die Kriegsschiffe haben verhältnismäszig wenig gelitten.

Drill (continued)

protects hospital ships. 6. That submarine is 250 feet long. 7. It can cruise on the surface at a speed of seventeen knots.

XVII

Heavy and Light Artillery

1. An army always needs the support of heavy artillery.

2. Both in advancing against hostile positions in the field and in attacks on fortresses it is of decisive importance.

3. The great guns, called field howitzers, are each drawn by six heavy draught horses.

4. Many are now also drawn by tractors.

5. This type of howitzer is a high-angle piece and has a caliber about twice the size of field artillery cannon.

6. Mortars are another kind of heavy artillery with a still larger caliber but less mobile.

7. They are especially effective against concrete coverings and armored forts.

8. Both hurl a large shell provided with a contact fuse and filled with a strong explosive charge.

9. Upon bursting this shell throws a large quantity of effective fragments in all directions.

10. No fortification yet built has been able to stand such a bombardment for any length of time.

XVII

1. Eine Armee braucht immer die Unterstützung der schweren Artillerie.
2. Im Vorrücken gegen feindliche Stellungen im Felde sowohl wie in dem Angriff auf Festungen ist sie von ausschlaggebender Bedeutung.
3. Die groszen Geschütze, Feldhaubitzen genannt, werden je von sechs schweren Zugpferden gezogen.
4. Manche werden jetzt auch von Kraftmaschinen gezogen.
5. Diese Art Feldhaubitze ist ein Steilfeuergeschütz und hat ein Kaliber fast zweimal so grosz wie das einer Kanone der Feldartillerie.
6. Die Mörser bilden eine andere Art der schweren Geschütze mit einem noch gröszeren Kaliber aber weniger beweglich.
7. Sie sind besonders erfolgreich gegen Betondecken und Panzeranlagen.
8. Beide schleudern eine grosze Granate mit einem Aufschlagszünder versehen und mit einer starken Sprengladung gefüllt.
9. Beim Krepieren schleudert diese Granate eine ganze Menge wirksamer Sprengstücke nach allen Seiten.
10. Keine bis jetzt gebaute Festung hat solche Beschieszung auf die Dauer aushalten können.

11. The light artillery is much more mobile than the heavy artillery and is able to support the infantry more quickly.

12. The battery commander has the battery unlimber and shoot from cover.

13. After the infantry has advanced he orders the horses hitched to the guns again and an advance at a gallop.

14. In this way the light artillery keeps on advancing and helps drive the enemy backwards.

15. If it is necessary it can also cover the retreat of its own infantry.

16. In modern warfare both heavy and light artillery have had to fire from covered positions.

17. It has been necessary to protect them from the enemy's aeroplanes.

18. In the front trenches machine guns and mine throwers and also hand grenades are much used.

19. Another favorite weapon is the armored car or "tank".

20. This is an invention used for the first time last year.

DRILL

1. Heavy artillery supports the infantry. 2. The large guns are each drawn by six horses. 3. The howitzer is a high-angle gun. 4. Mortars are able to destroy concrete works. 5. The shell fired by

11. Die Feldartillerie ist viel beweglicher als die schwere Artillerie und kann die Infanterie schneller unterstützen.

12. Der Batterieführer läszt die Batterie abprotzen und aus gedeckter Stellung schieszen.

13. Nachdem die Infanterie vorgerückt ist, befehlt er die Anspannung wieder und ein Aufmarsch im Galopp.

14. Auf diese Weise rückt die Feldartillerie immer weiter vorwärts und hilft den Feind zurückzudrängen.

15. Wo es nötig ist, kann sie auch den Rückzug der eigenen Infanterie decken.

16. In der modernen Kriegsführung haben die schwere Artillerie so wie die Feldartillerie aus gedeckter Stellung schieszen müssen.

17. Es ist nötig gewesen, sie vor den feindlichen Flugzeugen zu schützen.

18. In den vorderen Schützengräben werden Machinengewehre, Minenwerfer und auch Handgranaten viel gebraucht.

19. Noch eine beliebte Waffe ist der Panzerkraftwagen oder Tank.

20. Dieser ist eine Erfindung, welche voriges Jahr zum erstenmal gebraucht wurde.

Drill—(continued)

these guns explodes on contact. 6. The shell fragments are hurled in all directions.

XVIII

Infantry

1. More than two-thirds of the whole army consists of infantry.
2. In peace times the recruits are thoroughly drilled and then placed in the reserve army.
3. The most capable men are made reserve officers.
4. Firm discipline, marching ability, excellent shooting and skill are the characteristics of good infantry.
5. The company forms the center about which the larger infantry combinations are grouped.
6. The battalion, the regiment, the brigade, the division, the army corps are the larger divisions of the army in the field.
7. What the soldiers have learned in times of peace, in drill and in manoeuvers they must put into practice in war.
8. Before a long march the men must look carefully into the condition of their shoes and stockings.
9. It is hard to march in the heat and dust carrying gun and pack.
10. In the course of a twenty-five mile march the infantry must halt several times and rest.
11. Drinking water is fetched and the field kitchens attend to feeding the men.

XVIII

1. Mehr als zwei Drittel der gesamten Armee besteht aus Infanterie.

2. In Friedenszeiten werden die Rekruten tüchtig ausgebildet und dann in die Reserve gestellt.

3. Die tüchtigsten werden Reserveoffiziere.

4. Straffe Disziplin, grosze Marschleistungen, vorzügliches Schieszen und Gewandtheit sind die Eigenschaften einer guten Infanterie.

5. Die Kompagnie bildet den Mittelpunkt, um den sich die gröszeren Infanterieverbände gruppieren.

6. Das Bataillon, das Regiment, die Brigade, die Division und das Armeekorps sind die gröszeren Abteilungen des Feldheers.

7. Was die Soldaten im Frieden in den Gefechtsübungen und in dem Manöver gelernt haben, müssen sie im Kriege praktisch verwenden.

8. Vor einem langen Marsch müssen die Soldaten ihr Fuszeug ordentlich nachsehen.

9. Es ist schwer in der Hitze und in dem Staub mit Gewehr und Gepäck zu marschieren.

10. Im Laufe eines Marsches von fünfundzwanzig Kilometer musz das Fuszvolk mehrmals Rast halten.

11. Trinkwasser wird geholt, und die Feldküchen sorgen für die Verpflegung der Soldaten.

12. Tomorrow we shall pass the boundary and enter the enemy's territory.

13. "Forward" is the watch-word!

14. The infantry will "dig in" near the village of B.

15. An advance of the enemy against our right wing seems probable.

16. However, the infantry is there supported strongly by artillery and cavalry.

17 Two regiments of light cavalry of five companies each are at the disposition of the general.

18. The heavy cavalry is stationed on the left wing near the town of A.

19. The care of the horses in this part of the country is very difficult as fodder is so hard to procure.

20. When the artillery and the infantry have broken the hostile lines the cavalry will pursue the fleeing enemy.

DRILL

1. Infantry recruits learn firm discipline in times of peace. 2. They must also be able to shoot and march well. 3. The most capable men hope to become officers of the reserve. 4. We shall have a long march to-morrow. 5. Look well to your foot wear. 6. Drinking water and food will be pro-

12. Morgen werden wir die Grenze überschreiten und in des Feindes Land einziehen. .

13. Vorwärts heiszt die Parole!

14. Die Infanterie wird sich bei dem Dorf B verschanzen.

15. Ein Vormarsch des Feindes gegen unsern rechten Heeresflügel scheint wahrscheinlich.

16. Aber dort hat die Infanterie starke Unterstützung seitens der Artillerie und der Kavallerie.

17. Zwei Regimenter Husaren zu je fünf Schwadronen stehen dem General zur Verfügung.

18. Die schwere Kavallerie, Ulanen und Kürassiere, hat ihre Stellung auf dem linken Flügel bei der Stadt A.

19. Die Verpflegung der Pferde in diesem Teil des Landes macht grosze Schwierigkeiten, weil es so schwer ist, Futter zu kriegen.

20. Wenn die Artillerie und die Infanterie die feindliche Linie durchbrochen haben, wird die Kavallerie den fliehenden Feind verfolgen.

Drill—(continued)

vided. 7. Where is the heavy cavalry stationed? 8. Are we going to advance against the enemy's right wing? 9. We intrenched yesterday near the city of A. 10. The light cavalry is following up the retreating enemy.

XIX

MILITARY RANK

1. The supreme command over all the military forces of Germany is held by the federal commander-in-chief, the German Emperor.
2. At his side stand the field marshals and the highest staff officers.
3. There follow the generals of the infantry, artillery and cavalry as commanding officers of the various army corps.
4. The lieutenant general leads a division and the major general a brigade.
5. Other higher officers are the colonel, who commands the regiment, the lieutenant-colonel, the major and the captain.
6. As subaltern officers the first lieutenant and the two second lieutenants lead the three sections of a company.
7. The non-commissioned officers consist of the sergeant-majors, the sergeants and the corporals.
8. The more capable common soldiers often serve at times as corporals.
9. Soldiers in their first year are called recruits.
10. Men of education may volunteer and they are called one-year-volunteers.
11. In peace times the educated man has to serve in the army only one year.

XIX

1. Der Oberbefehl über die ganze Heeresmacht Deutschlands führt der Bundesfeldherr, der Deutsche Kaiser.
2. Ihm zur Seite stehen die General-Feldmarschalle und die höchsten Stabsoffiziere.
3. Es folgen dann die Generale der Infanterie, der Artillerie und der Kavallerie als Kommandierende Generale der verschiedenen Armeekorps.
4. Der Generalleutnant führt eine Division und der Generalmajor eine Brigade.
5. Andere höhere Offiziere sind der Oberst, der ein Regiment führt, der Oberstleutnant, der Major und der Kapitän.
6. Als Subalternoffiziere führen der Oberleutnant und zwei Leutnants die drei Züge einer Kompagnie.
7. Die Unteroffiziere bestehen aus den Feldwebeln, den Vizefeldwebeln und den eigentlichen Unteroffizieren.
8. Die tüchtigeren gemeinen Soldaten dienen oft bisweilen als Gefreite.
9. Soldaten in dem ersten Dienstjahr werden Rekruten genannt.
10. Gebildete Männer dürfen sich freiwillig melden und dann heiszen sie Einjährige Freiwillige.
11. In Friedenszeiten hat der gebildete Mann blosz ein Jahr im Heere zu dienen.

12. The uneducated man must serve for two years at least.
13. The auxiliary troops of the army are also divided into regiments, battalions, companies, etc.
14. The duty of these troops is to build bridges and railroads and lay telephone and telegraph wires, etc.
15. The train attends to the transportation of ammunition, food and baggage.
16. The medical corps attends to everything connected with the sick and wounded.
17. (a) Fall in! (b) Fall out! (c) Attention! (d) Right dress! (e) Count off!
18. (a) Rest! (b) Right face! Left face! (c) Forward, march! (d) Halt! (e) Mark time!
19. (a) Right (left) turn! (b) To the rear, march! (c) Right (left) oblique, march! (d) Right (left) by squads, march! (e) Route order, march!
20. (a) Lead out! (b) Mount! Dismount! (c) Trot, march! Gallop, march! Walk, march! (d) By the right (left) flank, march! (e) Right (left) by squads, march!

DRILL

1. The educated man in Germany can volunteer and then needs to serve only one year in the army. 2. He can become an officer of the reserve. 3. Have you seen the infantry general? 4. Who are the

12. Der Ungebildete musz mindestens zwei Jahre dienen.

13. Die Spezialwaffen oder Hilfstruppen zerfallen auch in Regimenter, Bataillone und Kompagnieen.

14. Die Aufgabe dieser Truppen ist, Brücken und Eisenbahnen zu bauen und Telephonen-und Telegraphenanlagen zu besorgen.

15. Der Train besorgt das Herschaffen von Munitionen, Verpflegung und Gepäck.

16. Das Sanitätskorps hat Aufsicht über alles, was die Kranken und Verwundeten betrifft.

17. (a) Antreten! (Angetreten!) (b) Abtreten. (c) Stillgestanden! (d) Richtet euch! (e) Abzählen.

18. (a) Rührt euch! (b) Rechts um! Links um! (c) Vorwärts, marsch! (d) Halt! (e) Auf der Stelle, marsch!

19. (a) Rechts (links) schwenkt, marsch! (b) Kehrt, marsch! (c) Halb rechts (links), marsch! (d) In Sektionen rechts (links), brecht ab! (e) Ohne Tritt, marsch!

20. (a) Pferde vor! (b) Aufgesessen! Abgesessen! (c) Trab, marsch! Galopp, marsch! Schritt, marsch! (d) Rechts (links) um, marsch! (e) In Sektionen rechts (links), marsch!

Drill—(continued)

officers of your company? 5. Our regiment is led by Colonel B.

XX
MAPS—MILITARY INFORMATION

1. We must provide ourselves with special maps of the hostile territory.

2. It would be much better, if we could have a topographical sketch of that district.

3. Send out a detail of men and have them make a road map of the country between A and B.

4. The scale should be one centimeter for each five kilometers.

5. Lieutenant N has a splendid military map of the region around B.

6. It has squares of five square miles each and the contour lines represent a difference in elevation of ten feet.

7. The shading is good and the conventional signs are attached.

8. For the artillery a panoramic sketch is needed.

9. Take a plane table with compass, paper, pencil, etc. with you and make a sketch of this sector.

10. You will also need an eraser, a penknife and a ruler.

11. One of our aviators has brought back some photographs of the territory immediately behind the enemy's lines.

XX

1. Wir müssen uns mit Spezialkarten des feindlichen Landes versehen.

2. Es wäre viel besser, wenn wir eine topographische Skizze von der Gegend haben könnten.

3. Schicken Sie ein kleines Detachement Leute hinaus und lassen Sie sie eine gute Wegskizze von dem Gelände zwischen A und B machen.

4. Der Maszstab sollte ein Centimeter für alle fünf Kilometer sein.

5. Leutnant N hat eine vorzügliche Kriegskarte von der Gegend um B.

6. Sie hat ein Netz von je fünf Quadratkilometer, und die Höhenkurven stellen einen Höhenunterschied von drei Meter dar.

7. Die Schraffierung ist gut, und die üblichen Bezeichnungen sind beigegeben.

8. Für die Artillerie ist eine Panoramaskizze nötig.

9. Nehmen Sie einen Mesztisch mit Deklinatorium, Papier, Bleistift usw. mit und machen Sie eine Skizze von diesem Sektor.

10. Sie werden auch ein Radiergummi, ein Federmesser und ein Lineal brauchen.

11. Einer von unseren Fliegern hat einige Photographieen von dem Terrain gerade hinter der feindlichen Linie zurückgebracht.

12. If you compare these with the map you can see the effect of yesterday's bombardment.

13. At headquarters they have a large collection of maps and photographs showing the position of the troops along the whole front.

14. The general staff must study these maps and work out new plans.

15. When prisoners are taken they are brought before an officer who questions them.

16. When many are questioned, something is often learned of the intended offense of the enemy.

17. Letters and diaries found on the prisoners are also read carefully for the information they may contain.

18. Aviators can also usually observe the movements of large masses of troops.

19. In the front trenches there are so called listening posts where sentries listen for the slightest sound in the opponent's lines.

20. Through these means it is often possible to discover the intentions of the enemy.

DRILL

1. I wish we had a better road map of this district. 2. Have you a plane table and the other things necessary for making one? 3. Lieutenant N has a fine map on which the contour lines are very clear. 4. Sergeant B will make a panoramic sketch of this sector. 5. What sort of photo-

12. Wenn man diese mit der Karte vergleicht, kann man den Erfolg der gestrigen Beschieszung sehen.

13. In dem groszen Hauptquartier hat man eine grosze Sammlung von Karten und Photographieen, welche die Truppenstellungen an der ganzen Front zeigen.

14. Der Generalstab musz diese Karten studieren und neue Pläne ausarbeiten.

15. Wenn Gefangene gemacht werden, bringt man sie vor einen Offizier, der sie ausfragt.

16. Wenn viele ausgefragt werden, lernt man oft etwas von den Angriffsabsichten des Feindes.

17. Briefschaften und Tagebücher der Gefangenen werden auch sorgfältig durchgelesen wegen der Auskunft, die sie vielleicht enthalten.

18. Flieger können auch gewöhnlich die Bewegungen von groszen Truppenmassen beobachten.

19. In den vordersten Schützengräben gibt es sogenannte Hörposten, wo die Wachen auf das leiseste Geräusch in den Linien des Gegners aufpassen.

20. Durch diese Mittel ist es oft möglich, die Absichten des Feindes zu entdecken.

Drill—(continued)

graphs did the aviator bring back with him? 6. What does the General Staff do with its collection of maps? 7. Did you read all those letters and diaries of the prisoners yesterday?

VOCABULARY

THIS vocabulary, (or more properly, word list) is not exhaustive and contains only the more important words and phrases used in the text exercises. The customary abbreviations are used. A dash (—) stands for the repetition of the title-word.

Inseparable compound verbs are printed as one word (*beschieszen*). Separable compound verbs are printed with a hyphen (*an-treten*). Strong and irregular verbs are marked with an asterisk (*).

In general only the meanings which occur in the text are given.

A

ability, Tüchtigkeit f.
able, to be—, können*.
about, *adv.* ungefähr,
accommodations, afford—for, beherbergen.
accompany, begleiten.
account, Rechnung, f. —en.
admittance, Eingang, m.⸺e; Eintritt, m.—e.; No—! Eintritt Verboten!
advance, vor-rücken.
afflicted, behaftet.
aiming point, Zielpunkt, m.-e.
air, Luft, f. ⸺e; —man, Flieger, m.-; —plane, Flugzeug, n.-e.
ambulance Ambulanz, f.—en.
ammunition, Munition, f. -en.
angle of departure, Abgangswinkel, m.—.
announce, melden; —ment, Bekanntmachung, f. —en.
anti-aircraft cannon, Ballonkanone, f. —n.
apply to, sich wenden* an (*acc.*)
armored train, Panzerzug, m. ⸺e; cruiser, Panzerkreuzer, m.—.
army, Heer, n. —e.
arrive, an-kommen*, ein-treffen*
artillery, heavy —, schwere Artillerie, f.; light —, Feldartillerie, f.

assist, behilflich sein.*
attack, *n.* Angriff, m. —e.; counter —, Gegen —.
attack, *v.* an-greifen.*
attempt, Versuch, m. —e.
attend to, besorgen.
attention, call — to, aufmerksam machen auf (*acc.*).
aviator, Flieger, m. —.

B

bank (*of stream*), Ufer, n.—.
battery, Batterie, f. —en.; —commander, Batteriechef, m. —s.; —telescope, Batteriefernrohr, n. —e.
battle, Schlacht, f.—en.; -ship, Linienschiff, n. —e.
bean, Bohne, f. —n.
become, werden*.
begin, an-fangen*.
bell, Glocke, f. —n.
belong, gehören.
bid, heiszen*.
blanket, Decke, f. —n.
blockade, Blockade, f. —n.; to declare a —, in Blockadezustand erklären.
blow up (*bridges, etc.*), sprengen.
bomb, Bombe, f. —n.
bombard, beschieszen*; (*from airplane*) mit Bomben bewerfen*.

bookseller, Buchhändler, m.—.
booty, Beute, f.
border, Grenze, f. —n.
branch, Zweig, m. —e.
brass, Messing, n.
brave, wacker.
bread, Brot, n. —e.
breath, Atem, m.
bridge, Brücke, f. —n.; — of battleship, Kommandobrücke f. —n.
bright, blank.
bring along, mit-bringen*.
building, Gebäude, n. —.
burst, sprengen.
button, Knopf, m. ⸚e.

C

call for dinner, "alle Mann mittag."
cannon, Geschütz, n. —e.
capable, tüchtig.
captain, Hauptmann, m. pl. Hauptleute.
captive balloon, Fesselballon, m. —s.
capture, Einnahme, f. —n.
care, Verpflegung, f.; take — of, pflegen.
careful, Be —! Vorsicht!
cargo, Ladung, f. —en.
carry, tragen*.
cavalry, Kavallerie, f.; light —, Husaren; heavy —, Uhlanen.

certificate of vaccination, Impfschein, m. —e.
change, (=*alter*), ändern.
cheap, billig.
cheese, Käse, m. —.
chief advantage, Hauptvorteil, m. —e.
clear, klar.
coast, Küste, f. —n.
collection, Sammlung, f. —en.
colonel, Oberst, m. —en.
color, Farbe, f. —n.
comfortable, behaglich.
commander, Kommandant, m. —en.
company, Kompagnie, f.—en.
concrete works, Betondecke, f. —n.
confiscate, konfiszieren, ein-ziehen*.
contact, Aufprall, m.
contain, enthalten*.
continue, fort-fahren*.
contour line, Höhenkurve, f. —n.
contradict, widersprechen*.
contrary, on the —, im Gegenteil.
convalescence, *f.* Genesung,
corner, Ecke, f. —n.
correct, richtig.
count off, ab-zählen.
country, Land, n. ⸚er.

course, in the — of, im Laufe von.
cover, decken.
crew, Besatzung, f. —en.
cross (*stream, etc.*), überschreiten*.
cruise, fahren*.
cruiser, Kreuzer, m. —.

D

danger, Gefahr, f. —en.
dangerous, gefährlich.
deck gun, Deckgeschütz, n. -e.
declare, erklären.
defence, Verteidigung, f. —en.
deflection, Abweichung, f. —en.
delayed, verzögert.
departure, angle of —, Abgangswinkel, m. —.
depend upon, ab-hangen* von; (=*rely on*), sich verlassen* auf (*acc.*).
description, Beschreibung, f. —en.
despatch, Depesche, f. —n.
destroy, zerstören.
determine, übersehen lassen*; fest-stellen.
diary, Tagebuch, n. ⸚er.
dictionary, Wörterbuch, n. ⸚er.
dinner, call for —, "alle Mann mittag."
direction, Seite, f. —n; in the — of, nach...zu.

dirigible, lenkbar.
discharge, entlassen*.
discipline, Disziplin, f.
discover, entdecken.
disease, Krankheit, f. —en. (*see special list p.17*)
disorder, Unordnung, f. —en.
disperse, zerstreuen.
disposal, Verfügung, f. —en.
distance, Ferne, f.
district, Gegend, f. —en.
doctor, Arzt, m. ⸚e.
draw, ziehen*.
dress, sich an-ziehen*.
drinking water, Trinkwasser, n. —.
drive, Vorstosz, m. ⸚e.
drive back, zurück-drängen.
drop, fallen lassen*.
due, fällig.
dugout, Unterstand, m. ⸚e.
duty, Pflicht, f. —en.

E

early, früh.
easy, leicht.
educated, gebildet.
efficient., tüchtig.
egg, Ei, n. —er.
employ (=*use*), an-wenden*.
enable, befähigen.
enemy, Feind, m. —e.; *adj.*, feindlich.

engage in, teil-nehmen *an (*dat.*)
enough, genug.
enter (=*take up*), auf-nehmen*.
equal to, gewachsen.
equip, aus-rüsten, versehen*.
escape, entgehen*.
especial, besonder.
example, for —, zum Beispiel.
expensive, teuer.
explicit, ausführlich.
explode, sprengen.
extinguish, löschen.

F

fail (*of attack, etc.*), scheitern.
fall in, an-treten.*.
familiar with, bekannt mit.
famous, berühmt.
far, weit.
fast, schnell.
favorite, beliebt.
feed, füttern.
fetch, holen.
field ambulance service, Feldambulanzdienst, m. —e.
fight, Kampf, m. ⸚e.
find out, ausfindig machen.
fine, vorzüglich.
firm, straff.
fit for service, dienstfähig.
fleet, Flotte, f. —n.

flight, Flug, m. ⸚e.
fluently, geläufig.
fly, fliegen*.
flying craft, Flugzeug, m. —e.
follow, folgen; —up, verfolgen.
food, Verpflegung, f.
foothold, obtain a —, Fusz fassen.
footwear, Fuszzeug, m.
forces (*fighting* —), Streitkräfte, *pl.*
fort, Fort, n. —s.
fortification, Festung, f. —en.
forward, vorwärts;—movement, Vorwärtsbewegung, f. —en.
fragment, Splitter, m. —.
fresh, frisch.
front, Front(e), f. —n.

G

garrison, Besatzung, f. —en.
gas mask, Gasmaske, f. —n.
gay, bunt.
general, General, m. —e; —staff, Generalstab, m.
get, bekommen*.
give up, auf-geben*.
graze, Aufprall, m.; on —, beim —.
gun, (=*cannon*), Geschütz, n. —e.

H

halt, halten*.
ham, Schinken, m. —.
hand, Hand, f. ⸚e; —grenade, Handgranate, f. —n.
hangar, Luftschiffhalle, f. —n.
harbor, Hafen, m. ⸚.
hard, schwer.
headquarters (*army*), Heeresleitung, f.
health, Gesundheit, f. —en.
hear, hören.
heavy, schwer.
high angle gun, Steilfeuergeschütz, n. —e.
hill, Hügel, m. —.
hit, treffen*.
hope, hoffen.
horse, Pferd, n. —e.
hospital, Lazarett, n. —e.; —ship, Krankenschiff, n. —e.
howitzer, Haubitze, f. —n.
hurl, schleudern.
hurry, Eile, f.

I

infantry, Infanterie, f.
impend, bevor-stehen*.
importance, Bedeutung, f.
infer, schlieszen*.
injure (*objects*), beschädigen.
injury (*wound*), Verletzung, f. —en.

ink, Tinte, f. —n.
insignificant, gering.
insist on, bestehen* auf (*dat*).
intend, beabsichtigen.
intention, Absicht, f. —en.
intercept, auf-fangen*.
international law, Völkerrecht, n.
interrupt, unterbrechen*.
intrench, sich verschanzen.

K

keep, behalten*.
key, Schlüssel, m. —.
knapsack, Tornister, m. —.
knot, Knoten, m. —.
know (*facts*), wissen*; (*persons and things*) kennen*; (*languages, etc.*) können*; —one's way around, Bescheid wissen*.

L

lame., *v.* lähmen.
lay down (*arms*), strecken.
lead, führen; (*mil*) an-führen.
learn, lernen.
leave, *n.* Urlaub, m. —e.
leave, *v.* (*trains* —, *etc.*) ab-fahren*.
left, link.
letter, Brief, m. —e; (*collective*), Briefschaften.
light, Licht, n. —er. adj. leicht.

line, Linie, f. —n.; contour —, Höhenkurve, f. —n.
long, lang; be —, Länge haben.
look up (*in books*), nachschlagen*.

M

machine gun, Maschinengewehr, n. —e.
mail, Post, f. —en.
manoeuver, Übung, f. —en.
map, Landkarte, f. —n.
march, n. Marsch, m. ⸚e.
march, v. marschieren.
martial law, Kriegsrecht, n.
mask, Maske, f. —n.
mayor, Bürgermeister, m. —.
meat, Fleisch, n. —e.
medical corps, Sanitätscorps, n.
mess kit, Kochgeschirr, n. —e.
military, Militär, m. —e.
mine explosion, Minensprengung, f. —en.
mine thrower, Minenwerfer, m. —.
miss (*train, etc.*), verpassen.
mistake, make a —, sich irren.
mobilization, Mobilisierung, f. —en.
month, Monat, m. —e.
mortar, Mörser, m. —.
motor, Motor, m. —en.
moved, beweglich.
"movies", Kinos, pl.
muffler, Halstuch, n. ⸚er.

N

name, what is your —? wie heiszen Sie; by the —of, namens.
necessary, nötig.
need, brauchen.
negotiations for surrender, Übergabeverhandlungen.
neutral, neutral.
newspaper, Zeitung, f. —en.
number, Zahl, f. —en.
numbers (=*mass*), Menge, f.-n.

O

occur, vor-kommen*.
offensive, *n.* Offensive, f. —n.
officer, Offizier, m. —e.; —of the reserve, Reserveoffizier.
official, *adj.* amtlich.
oil, Öl, n. —e.
once, at —, sofort.
only, blosz, nur.
opinion, Ansicht, f. —en.
over (=*past*), vorbei; (=*beyond*), über.
outer, äuszer.
over there, da drüben.

84

P

ackage, Paket, n. —e.
anoramic sketch, Panoramaskizze, f. —n.
ardon, Verzeihung, f. —en.
art, Teil, m. —e.
assenger, Passagier, m. —e.
ay, bezahlen, (*in advance*= im voraus).
eace, Friede, m. —n.
enetrate, ein-dringen* in (*acc*).
ercentage, Prozent, n. —e.
eriscope, Periskop, n. —e.
hotograph, Photographie, f. —en.
ilot, Führer, m. —.
lain, einfach.
lane table, Mesztisch, m. —e.
oint, Punkt, m. —e.
osition, Stellung, f. —en.
ossession, Besitz, m. —e.; take — of, sich bemächtigen (*gen*).
otato, Kartoffel, f. —n.
ractice, Übung, f. —en.; target —, Schieszübung.
raise, loben.
repared, bereit.
retend, sich stellen.
risoner, Gefangener (*adj. infl.*) —of war, Kriegs —.
robably, wahrscheinlich.
rotect, schützen.

proud, stolz (*of*= *auf w. acc.*)
provide, besorgen.
provision column, Proviantkolonne, f. —n.

Z

question, Frage, f. —n. (*ask*= stellen).

R

railroad troops, Eisenbahner, m. —
range finder, Entfernungsmesser, m. —.
(X)ray, (X-)Strahl, m. —en.
ready, fertig.
rear (*to the* —), kehren.
receipt, quittieren.
recommend, empfehlen*.
regiment, Regiment, n. —er.
region, Bezirk, m. —e.
remote, entfernt, zurückgelegen.
report, *n.* Bericht, m. —e.
report, *v.* berichten; (=*announce oneself*), sich melden.
repulse, zurück-werfen*.
reserve, Reserve f. —n.
rest, sich aus-ruhen.
resume work, an-treten*.
return, zurück-kehren.
right, recht; all —, schön, schon gut.

road map, Wegskizze, f. —n.
roastbeef, Rindfleisch, n.
route (*order*), ohne Tritt.

S

sacrifice, Opfer, n. —.
sail, aus-laufen*.
sausage, Wurst, f. ⸚e.
search, untersuchen.
sector, Abschnitt, m. —e.; Sektor, m. —en.
see to, sorgen für.
sentry, Wache, f. —n.
service, Dienst, m. —e.
shell, Granate, f. —n.; — fragment, Granatsplitter, m. —.
shelter, unterbringen*.
shiny, blank.
ship, Schiff, n. —e.
shoot, schieszen*.
short, kurz.
shot, Schusz, m. ⸚e.; Geschosz, n. —e.
sign, Aufschrift, f. —en.; Anschlag, m. ⸚e.
silence, zum Schweigen bringen*
site, Erhöhungswinkel, m. —.
situation, Lage, f. —n.
soldier, Soldat, m. —en.
sort, what — of, was für.
sound, n. Geräusch, n. —e.
sound, v. (= *strike*), schlagen*.
soup, Suppe, f. —n.

speed, Geschwindigkeit, f. —en.
spread (*diseases* —), um sich greifen*.
squad, Sektion, f. —en.
station, stellen; Stellung haben.
steamer, Dampfer, m. —.
still, keep —, schweigen*.
stop, auf-halten.*
strange(r), fremd.
strategic, strategisch.
strong, stark.
study, treiben*, lernen.
stupid, dumm.
submarine, Unterseeboot, n.-e
succeed, gelingen*. (*impers.*).
success, Erfolg, m. —e.
successful, erfolgreich.
superior, überlegen.
support, unterstützen.
surface, Oberfläche, f. —n.; on the —, aufgetaucht.
surrender, sich ergeben*.
surroundings, Umgebung, f. —en.

T

talk, reden.
tank, Tank, m.; Panzerkraftwagen, m. —.
target, Ziel, n. —e.; Scheibe, f. —n.; —practice, Schieszübung, f. —en.

territory, Gebiet, n. —e.
theater of war, Kriegsschauplatz, m. ⁻e.
threatening, drohend.
torpedo, Torpedo, m. —s.
torpedo boat, Torpedoboot, n. —e.
train, Zug, m. ⁻e.
transportation, Transport, m.
translate, übersetzen.
trench, Schützengraben, m. ⁻.
troops, Truppen (*pl.*).
turn, sich wenden*.

U

unconditionally, auf Gnade und Ungnade.
unterstand, verstehen*.
understood, make oneself —, sich verständlich machen.
uniform, Uniform, f. —en.
use, Gebrauch, m. ⁻e.
useful, nützlich.

V

vegetables, Gemüse, n.
view, Aussicht, f. —en.
village, Dorf, n. ⁻er.

violent, heftig.
volunteer, sich freiwillig melden.

W

water, *v.* tränken.
way, Weg. m. —e.; lose one's —, sich verirren.
weapon, Waffe, f. —n.
wear, tragen*.
week, Woche, f. —n.
well (=*carefully*), ordentlich.
what sort of, was für.
wing, Flügel, m. —.
woolen, wollen.
work, resume —, wieder antreten*.
writing paper, Schreibpapier, n. —e.

Y

yard, Elle, f. —n.—(*Meter, m.*— =1.0936 *yds.*).
yesterday, gestern.

87